POV Press
Books by Bethanne Kim

Survival Skills for All Ages:
　　#1: 26 Basic Life Skills
　　#2: 52⁺ Everyday Recipes for Emergencies
　　#3: 26 Mental and Urban Life Skills

Scouting in the Deep End:
　　#1: Cubmastering: Getting Started as Cubmaster
　　#2: Scout Leader: An Introduction to Boy Scouts
　　#3: Citizenship in the World: Teaching the Merit Badge

Not the Zombies:
　　#1: OMG!
　　#2: BRB!
　　#3: YOLO!

The Constitution: It's the OS for the US

The Organized Wedding: Planning Everything from Your Engagement to Your Marriage

Forthcoming:

Survival Skills for All Ages:
　　26 Outdoor Life Skills
　　Special Needs Prepping

Scouting in the Deep End:
　　#4: Mentoring Youth in Scouts

Citizenship in the World
Teaching the Merit Badge

Bethanne Kim

(a dumped-in-the-deep-end Scouter)

Cover Photo by NASA (Apollo 10, May 18, 1969)

1. Non-fiction–Family & Relationships–Education
2. Non-fiction–Political Science–Civics & Citizenship

ISBN: 978-1-942533-11-5

Distributed by POV Press
PO Box 399
Catharpin, VA 20143

Printed in the United States of America

Foreword

I *hate* not being prepared. Seriously, I can't stand it. When I agreed to be a Merit Badge Counselor for Citizenship in the World for my son's troop, the first thing I did was to sit through an entire class of someone else teaching it. The second was to search online for resources I could use. I found an outline online that looked great and was, truly, a big help. But I still needed more to feel confident in presenting the class.

That's where this book came into being. Some of the original framework I found online is still in here but everything has been researched, reviewed, updated, rewritten, and (when appropriate) linked. The first time I presented this material, I noticed that the boys became much more engaged whenever dictators where discussed. While it could be a quirk of the youth I'm around, I'm guessing it isn't, so I have tried to work dictators and failed states in whenever it's reasonable.

The design and intention of this book is that a merit badge counselor should be able to pick it up and teach the class with little to no preparation beyond what is included in this short book. Audio-visual aids always help make presentations more interesting. In this case, clothing and other items from countries being discussed helps keep them interested, taking care to avoid stereotypes and being inflammatory (even a little bit) when discussing other cultures.

Sharing passports (they don't need to be yours) can also be good. If you can find several from different decades, then you can show how they have become more secure (and harder to forge) over the years. I happened to have one with stamps from an Eastern Block country, one from before the USSR fell and one from after. Before the wall came down, it used a specific, harder-to-replicate multi-ink pattern. Afterward, just plain black ink. Actually holding and looking at this sort of thing is far more interesting than simply listening to a lecture or reading a Power-Point slide. But then, you already knew that from all the lectures and PowerPoint slides you have sat through!

It is my sincere hope that this helps you with teaching the Citizenship in the World merit badge.

Yours In Scouting (YiS),

Bethanne Kim

TABLE OF CONTENTS

(1)
CITIZENSHIP DISCUSSION

EXPLAIN WHAT CITIZENSHIP IN THE WORLD MEANS TO YOU AND WHAT YOU THINK IT TAKES TO BE A GOOD WORLD CITIZEN.

The website "Technology Student" has a good brief description and a worksheet to discuss characteristics of a good citizen. These include love for their own country, respect for other countries, following the law, contributing society/their community, and respecting authority.

www.technologystudent.com/PDF_PSE1/citizen3a.pdf

(2)
CITIZENSHIP

EXPLAIN HOW ONE BECOMES A CITIZEN IN THE UNITED STATES, AND EXPLAIN THE RIGHTS, DUTIES, OBLIGATIONS OF US CITIZENSHIP. DISCUSS THE SIMILARITIES AND DIFFERENCES BETWEEN THE RIGHTS, DUTIES, AND OBLIGATIONS OF US CITIZENS AND THE CITIZENS OF TWO OTHER COUNTRIES.

A **citizen** is a native or naturalized person who owes allegiance to a specific nation and is entitled to protection by its government.

A **subject** is a person ruled by a sovereign authority such as a monarch and expected to show loyalty to both the ruling authority and the nation.

Naturalization is the process of a non-citizen becoming a citizen. People are either natural-born or naturalized citizens. In the United States, the only positions a natural born citizen may have that a naturalized citizen may not are President and Vice-President. This is because a naturalized citizen may still have some feelings (positive or negative) toward their original nation and this could affect how they carry out the job of President of the United States (POTUS).

THE UNITED STATES OF AMERICA (DEMOCRATIC REPUBLIC)

There are four (4) different ways to become a US Citizen.

Birth:

The 14th Amendment states: **"All persons born or naturalized in the United States, and subject to the jurisdiction thereof, are citizens of the United States and of the State wherein they reside."** This is generally interpreted to mean that anyone born on US soil anywhere in the world, very specifically including both military and foreign service (diplomatic) locations, is automatically a US citizen, even if the newborn's parents aren't here legally. The clear exception to this a child whose parents are diplomats. Diplomats are not "subject to the jurisdiction" of the United States (or whatever country they are stationed in) because they have "diplomatic immunity" that specifically exempts them (discussed more in Requirement 6). That means their children are not US citizens from birth, and there is an argument that this may also apply to a child whose parents are not here legally, but that is not the current legal understanding.

Naturalization, Article I:

Section 8 states that the US Congress is responsible for establishing "uniform rule of naturalization." Rules for becoming a citizen are set by the central or federal government, not by states or provinces, and this is true for every country.

Once a person meets all the naturalization requirements, they can apply for naturalization. The US has multiple paths to naturalization including marrying a US citizen, joining the US military, and studying in the US.

Several months after the naturalization application is filed, Immigration and Customs Enforcement (ICE) sends applicants an interview notice. During the interview, ICE reviews the application to ensure all the citizenship answers are correct. They also test the applicant's English fluency, and understanding of US history and government.

US Naturalization Requirements:
https://www.uscis.gov/us-citizenship/citizenship-through-naturalization/path-us-citizenship

Derivative Citizenship:
When parents are naturalized, their non-citizen minor (under age 18) children may become citizens as well, if they are already in the country. These minor children derive their citizenship from their parents, so it is called "derivative" citizenship. Laws about "derivative citizenship" vary widely around the world.

This is a different reason than "birth" because it applies to children who already have citizenship from another nation. The child then gives up that citizenship and acquires US citizenship. With citizenship from birth, they only ever have US citizenship.

Acquired Citizenship:
A child might have "acquired" US citizenship at birth without the child or their parents knowing, if the child was born outside the US and at least one parent was a US citizen when the child was born. This might be true even if neither parent was born in the United Sates but one or more of the grandparents were.

This is an extremely complicated area of immigration law.

US RIGHTS
Citizens must obey the law, pay taxes, and, in many cases, serve in the armed forces for their government. In turn, the government provides physical safety and public services, and protects property. The following are the most basic rights enshrined in the Bill of Rights attached to the US Constitution. The Bill of Rights ensures that the US government protects these basic rights. Many, but not all, of these are guaranteed by other nations for their citizens as well.

- Voting
  - Voting is such a basic right that special accommodations allow astronauts to vote from space. NASA has the motto "vote while you float". Thanks to a 1997 Texas law, Mission Control in Houston can forward a secure electronic ballot to astronauts, which is returned to the County Clerk by email.

- The Constitution and Bill of Rights (1st Ten Amendments of the US Constitution)
  - The 1st Amendment established the freedoms of speech, press, petition, assembly, and religion.
  - The 2nd Amendment established state militias (now the National Guard) and guaranteed our right to bear arms (own and carry firearms).
  - The 3rd Amendment forbade the government from forcing citizens to house soldiers.
  - The 4th Amendment forbade unreasonable searches and seizures by the government.
  - The 5th Amendment guaranteed the right to a jury trial and to refuse to testify in court if what we say will or could prove we're guilty of a crime. It forbade double jeopardy, which is being tried twice for the same crime once a verdict has been given.
  - The 6th Amendment guaranteed the right to a speedy jury trial near where the crime was committed, to a lawyer even at government expense, and to be told immediately what crime we are charged with.
  - The 7th Amendment guaranteed that civil trials are also tried by a jury.
  - The 8th Amendment forbade excessive bail, excessive fines, and cruel and unusual punishment.
  - The 9th Amendment established that we have rights that are not listed in the Constitution.

o The 10th Amendment established that anything not specifically given to the federal government in the Constitution is the responsibility of the state governments (state sovereignty).

Laws and court rulings have added other rights, such as the right to privacy, over the years. Many of these, privacy in particular, are covered under the 9th Amendment.

US DUTIES AND OBLIGATIONS

- Vote.
- Follow the law.
- Pay taxes (income, sales, personal, etc.) at the federal, state, and local levels.
- Serve on a jury when called (jury duty).
- At age 18, male citizens must register with the Selective Service System for possible conscription into the armed forces, although there is currently no draft.

CUBA (COMMUNIST)

The Republic of Cuba has a Communist government that openly embraces socialism, communism, Marxism, and Leninism.

The Cuban Constitution outlines citizens' rights, duties, and obligations. Among other things, it guarantees free education and health care, prohibits private ownership of media companies, and allows for state oversight (control) of religious institutions.

http://www.constitutionnet.org/files/Cuba%20Constitution.pdf

CUBAN RIGHTS

- No private property, except small farmers.
- No private industry.
- The state (central government) organizes, directs, and controls the economic life of the nation.

- Everyone has the right to health care and protection, although there is no guarantee of the quality.
- Freedom of speech and the press in keeping with the objectives of socialist society. Exercise of those "freedoms" is regulated by law.
- Youth are guaranteed an education, although neither the subject nor the duration is specified.

CUBAN DUTIES AND OBLIGATIONS

- Work in a socialist society is a right and duty and a source of pride for every citizen.
- Every worker has the duty to faithfully carry out tasks assigned to him at his job. (They do not have the right to choose their job.)
- Obey the law, including regulations requiring all Cubans to perform military service.
- Defense of the socialist homeland is the greatest honor and supreme duty of every Cuban citizen.

GERMANY (PARLIAMENTARY DEMOCRACY)

Germany is a Republic with a parliamentary democracy. It has two houses in the legislature as well as an executive branch and a judicial branch. The head of state is their Chancellor and their current constitution was adopted in 1949, after World War II. It is called the "Basic Law" and was influenced by the occupying nations (United States, United Kingdom, France), which explains the similarities. Intended as a temporary document to be used until the two halves of the nation reunited and created a permanent one. Forty one years later, reunification was, at long last, a reality, but few changes to the Basic Law were needed when that happened.

It is worth thinking about how the events of World War II while you are discussing the German government. Those events clearly affected the writing of their constitution.

CITIZENSHIP

GERMAN RIGHTS

- The rule of law: everyone is equal in the eyes of the law.
- Freedom of speech, assembly, news media, and worship.
- Article 18 states: "Whoever abuses freedom of expression of opinion, in particular freedom of the press, freedom of teaching, freedom of assembly, freedom of association, privacy of posts [note: "post" has historically referred to postal mail, derisively called "snail mail" today] and telecommunications, property, or the right of asylum in order to combat the free democratic basic order, shall forfeit these basic rights."
- Non-discrimination policies mean that no one can be treated differently because of their political beliefs, religion, gender, or race.
- The right to conscientious objection to compulsory military service.
- "All state authority emanates from the people. It shall be exercised by the people by means of elections and voting and by specific legislative, executive and judicial organs."
- Article 20 states that "the Federal Republic of Germany is a democratic and socialist federal state. The Basic Law, however, does not enumerate specific social duties of the state. However, the state does not need to compensate by market value for property seized for the common good."

www.constitutionnet.org/country/constitutional-history-germany

GERMAN DUTIES AND OBLIGATIONS:

- Vote.
- Obey German and European Union laws.
- Pay taxes.
- Stay righteous.
- Learn about the German Government and the European Union, originally called the European Economic Community when the Treaty of Rome was signed in 1957. It was also

called the "Common Market" and Germany was a founding member.

- Nine months of military or hospital service.

(3)
WORLD EVENTS

Do both:

(A) PICK A CURRENT WORLD EVENT. IN RELATION TO THIS CURRENT EVENT, DISCUSS WITH YOUR COUNSELOR HOW A COUNTRY'S NATIONAL INTEREST AND ITS RELATIONSHIP WITH OTHER COUNTRIES MIGHT AFFECT AREAS SUCH AS ITS SECURITY, ITS ECONOMY, ITS VALUES, AND THE HEALTH OF ITS CITIZENS.

> **Note to Counselors:** Immigration is a big issue in Europe as well as the United States, but European history means the issues are different. Germany's actions during WWII mean that they enshrined certain rights for refugees in their Basic Law.
>
> France and Great Britain have both been colonial powers and their former colonies have caused some thorny immigration issues for them.

(B) SELECT A FOREIGN COUNTRY AND DISCUSS WITH YOUR COUNSELOR HOW ITS GEOGRAPHY, NATURAL RESOURCES, AND CLIMATE INFLUENCE

ITS ECONOMY AND ITS GLOBAL PARTNERSHIPS WITH OTHER COUNTRIES.

Note to Counselors: Comparing North and South Korea is very effective for this and plays nicely into requirement five on comparative politics. There are many great online resources. Appendix One has a list for anyone in a time crunch.

(4)

INTERNATIONAL LAW AND CONFLICT RESO-LUTION

DO TWO OF THE FOLLOWING THREE:

(A) EXPLAIN INTERNATIONAL LAW AND HOW IT DIFFERS FROM NATIONAL LAW. EXPLAIN THE ROLE OF INTERNATIONAL LAW AND HOW IN-TERNATIONAL LAW CAN BE USED AS A TOOL FOR CONFLICT RESOLUTION.

(The remaining options are included later in this section.)

INTERNATIONAL LAW

We need International Law because there are approximately 200 na-tions on Earth. Each one has sovereign (national) interests, but they depend on each other more all the time. In particular, even geograph-ically large nations such as the USA, China, Canada, and Russia need to trade for resources they don't have. Individual businesses do even more trading between and among nations.

Isolationist nations such as North Korea and Iran are increasingly finding that they really need a larger, stronger nation as an ally so they have access to outside resources, including markets for their goods. Even nations that are not genuinely friendly, such as China and the United States, find themselves economically interdependent.

As noted, every nation has a different set of national laws, but there are some General Principals of Law that all civilized nations. Examples of these general principals of fairness and justice include having an impartial judiciary and prohibiting double jeopardy (retrying something once the courts have decided on it). When something comes up in court that international law does not have provision for, international courts and tribunals rely on these general principals.

When peaceful international relations dissolve into conflicts, international law can be applied to stop the conflicts from escalating to aggression and war. Some of the causes of these conflicts include:

- Terrorism
- Environmental concerns, trade, and economics, which are often interconnected
    - Some nations refuse to follow expensive environmental regulations, making their goods unfairly cheap and creating environmental and health hazards (Google "China+recall").
    - "Trade wars" are an actual thing.

- Disease
    - One nation may pollute water or redirect it (including damming) so it never reaches another nation. That can have massive health and farming implications.
    - If a disease runs rampant in one nation, wildlife and migrants can carry it to neighboring nations (e.g., Zika, Ebola).

- Politics, religion, and culture.
    - Strict Muslim nations and Western nations have different views of how women, in particular should dress and conduct themselves in public. Saudi Arabia does

not allow women to drive and (in public) they may only show their face. Europe has topless beaches.

o Communist and capitalist nations clash because their political beliefs are antithetical.

o Some nations have a national religion, while others prohibit it. The theocracies of Vatican City and Saudi Arabia have very different policies, while most Communist nations are officially atheist. A caliphate is an Islamic stated headed by a caliph, who has absolute religious and political power within that nation.

- Unwritten customs cause conflicts on a national and international level. On an individual level, this is a major reason that diplomatic immunity makes sense.
- Some nations refuse to recognize laws that conflict with their customs.

Nations have joined together over the years and signed quite a few International conventions, treaties, executive agreements.

- **Geneva Convention:** This is a set of four (4) treaties regarding humanitarian treatment in war.
- **Hague Conventions of 1899 and 1907:** These are a series of international treaties and declarations negotiated at the International Peace Conferences held at The Hague in 1899 and 1907. War crimes, laws of war, and international adoption are just a few of the items covered.
- Multiple conventions and treaties protect different aspects of **international property,** including non-physical properties such as digital content, copyrights, and patents.
- Multiple conventions and treaties regulate **extradition** between and among countries. Extradition is returning a person from a country where they aren't accused of a crime to one where they are accused.

  o The US Constitution covers extradition between and among US states.

- o Edward Snowdon fled to nations that do not have extradition treaties with the US after releasing information classified by the US government. That is a crime in the US, but not in those countries.

- The 1979 Agreement Covering the Activities of States on the **Moon and Other Celestial Bodies**
  - o Those bodies may only be used for peaceful purposes. In other words, things like lasers on the moon or mars targeting other nations are prohibited.
  - o Their environments shall not be disrupted.
  - o The UN shall be told the location and reason for any station established on those bodies.
  - o The moon and any natural resources on it are the common heritage of mankind and an international agency will oversee the exploitation of those resources when the time comes.

MARITIME (ADMIRALTY) LAW

Admiralty law establishes rules of behavior on the high seas and in non-country areas such as the Arctic regions. The movie *The Martian* posits that it may apply on other planets, such as Mars.

- National boundaries include "**boundary waters**" that show exactly how far national boundaries extend from the edge of land.
  - o Without boundary waters, enemies could literally stand in the surf on a nation's beach to attack them and technically be in international waters.
  - o Beyond these boundary waters, the seas and oceans are not technically part of any nation and maritime law applies.
- Maritime law specifically addresses **piracy** on the high seas.

- o *Captain Phillips* is a 2013 movie starring Tom Hanks that shows modern piracy.
- o The nation of Somalia (near where Africa bulges the farthest east) is the current center of high seas piracy.
- o After the Revolutionary War Navy was dispersed, American merchant ships needed help fighting off the "Barbary pirates". The US Navy formed under President Jefferson for just that task.

- The UN issues International Maritime laws. These are enforced by the navies and coast guards of member nations because the UN doesn't have a navy.

NATIONAL LAW

- National laws are the rules and regulations that govern a specific nation.
  - o Nations have their own written or unwritten Constitution or other primary governing document or rules.
  - o Laws are written by the national legislature, such as a Congress or Parliament, or by a dictator.
  - o Throughout human history, national laws have been supported by taxes, courts, fines, prisons, and a vast bureaucracy.
  - o These are easier to enforce than international law because a large apparatus including police officers, judges, lawyers, etc. ensures compliance.

INTERNATIONAL CONFLICT RESOLUTION

International law depends on member nations for enforcement. International organizations such as the UN have little or no manpower of their own because they lack a national citizenry to call upon. Despite that, they have had successes. On June 10, 1967, Syria and Israel agreed to a UN-brokered cease-fire, ending the Middle East War.

- Extremely poor or corrupt nations may be unable, or unwilling, to enforce international law.
- Members may choose not to enforce international laws that go against their national economic or security interests.
- Nations may refuse to enforce international law so they can damage an enemy, such as by pouring toxic chemicals into a key waterway for another nation.
- Members may selectively enforce laws in a way that punishes other nations or specific groups, such as by only enforcing environmental regulations at manufacturing plants owned by foreign companies.
- The International Court of Justice of the UN is the main judiciary element for the UN and has fifteen judges.
  - It hears disputes submitted by nations.
  - It issues opinions on questions submitted by different agencies within the UN.
  - It is located in The Hague, Netherlands. The other five main agencies within the UN are all in NYC.

If an agreement can't be reached, escalation is a real possibility and may take different forms.

- **Retorsion** is when the action is similar to the offence (an eye for an eye), such as imposing tariffs in response to another nation imposing tariffs. Retorsion can be used to pressure another nation to reverse an unfriendly act, or simply to damage another nation.
  - If Russia were to round up all the known and suspected American spies, the US might do the same for all known and suspected Russian spies.
  - If Andoria threw out the Vulcan diplomats, Vulcan might, in turn, revoke the diplomatic status of the Andorian embassy's staff and send them packing.
- **Reprisals** are an act of force in response to an illegal action. If the act was committed without a precipitating illegal action,

then it could be, itself, a precipitating illegal action, but it is legal as a reprisal.

- o If your sibling hits you in the car and you hit them back, it's a reprisal and you may not get in as much trouble – *if* you are believed. If you hit them first, it's not a reprisal and you are in the wrong.
- o If a nation borrows money and refuses to repay the loan, the lending nation or institution could legally seize the property used to guarantee repayment.

- **War** is the last resort, especially when nuclear weapons are involved. The threat of war can be enough to force a nation to change its ways.

(B)USING RESOURCES SUCH AS MAJOR DAILY NEWSPAPERS, THE INTERNET (WITH YOUR PARENTS' PERMISSION), AND NEWS MAGAZINES, OBSERVE A CURRENT ISSUE THAT INVOLVES INTERNATIONAL TRADE, FOREIGN EXCHANGE, BALANCE OF PAYMENTS, TARIFFS, AND FREE TRADE. EXPLAIN WHAT YOU HAVE LEARNED. INCLUDE IN YOUR DISCUSSION AN EXPLANATION OF WHY COUNTRIES MUST COOPERATE IN ORDER FOR WORLD TRADE AND GLOBAL COMPETITION TO THRIVE.

Note to Counselors: This requirement is not discussed here because two, not all three, need to be done.

(C) SELECT TWO OF THE FOLLOWING ORGANIZATIONS AND DESCRIBE THEIR ROLE IN THE WORLD: THE UNITED NATIONS AND UNICEF; THE WORLD COURT; INTERPOL; WORLD OR-

GANIZATION OF THE SCOUT MOVEMENT; WORLD HEALTH ORGANIZATION; AMNESTY INTERNATIONAL; INTERNATIONAL COMMITTEE OF THE RED CROSS; CARE (COOPERATIVE FOR AMERICAN RELIEF EVERYWHERE), AND THE EUROPEAN UNION.

UNITED NATIONS:

- Goals:
    - o Maintain international peace and security.
    - o Promote cooperation in solving international problems:
        - ▪ Political
        - ▪ Economic
        - ▪ Social
        - ▪ Cultural
        - ▪ Humanitarian

- Key objectives for the 21st century:
    - o Promote the creation of independent and democratic societies.
    - o Protect human rights.
    - o Save children from starvation and disease (UNICEF).
    - o Provide relief assistance to refugees and disaster victims.
    - o Counter global crime, drugs, and disease.
    - o Assist countries devastated by war and the long-term threat of landmines.

- Human Rights Council, formerly the UN Commission on Human Rights:
    - o Established in 2006 to replace the 60 year old UN Commission on Human Rights

- o Works to highlight human rights abuses around the world, including genocide, so pressure can be brought to bear to end them.
- o Failures include electing Libya to head the Commission in 2003 and Sudan in 2004.
- o Some Commission members have miserable human rights records. These include China, Cuba, Zimbabwe, Russia, Saudi Arabia, Pakistan, Algeria, Syria, Libya, and Vietnam.

- Humanitarian Assistance:
  - o Successes:
    - Work with other relief organizations such as the International Red Cross (Haiti).
    - Provision of food, water, and shelter in areas hit by war, famine, or natural disasters (tsunami).
    - The World Food Program serves 110 million people in 80 countries.
    - The High Commissioner for Refugees protects 116 countries.

  - o Failures:
    - Human rights abuses by UN Peacekeepers (soldiers). See above re: member nations with miserable human rights records and the need to recruit personnel from member nations.
    - Mismanagement and "unethical conduct" by UN personnel in the Oil-for-Food Program allowed Saddam Hussein to keep money spent on oil that was meant for food, instead of actually buying the food as intended.

UNICEF (United National Children's Fund) and World Health Organization (WHO)

Saving Children from Starvation and Disease:

- Provides childhood vaccines for life-threatening illnesses.
- Critical in effort that has nearly eliminated smallpox and polio.
- Continues fight against measles and tetanus. While rarely deadly in highly developed areas, these can be very dangerous in areas that are impoverished or have little access to healthcare.
- Improves access to clean water, as well as general sanitation and hygiene.
- Provides education and prevention for HIV/ AIDS.
- Assists with nutrition education and providing improved nutrition.

World Organization of the Scout Movement

The roots of Scouting have grown among young people of all civilized countries and are developing more each day. It might be thought that if, in years to come, a considerable proportion of the future citizens of each nation forms part of this brotherhood, they will be joined by a bond of personal friendship and mutual understanding such as has never existed before, which will help to find a solution to terrible international conflicts. – Lord Baden Powell

- Founded in 1907.
- Headquartered in Geneva, Switzerland.
- Promotes Scouting world-wide by supporting expansion and development, especially as new nations form.
    - o Since the mid-1980s, thirty nations have joined or rejoined, especially in eastern and central Europe.
    - o Over 40 million members (all Scouts in the world) in 161 countries, including roughly 6 million Americans.

- o In many nations, Boy Scouts and Girl Scouts are the same organization.
- Promotes unity and understanding among Scouting programs in different nations.
- WOSM holds the World Scout Jamboree at a different location every four years to increase understanding, tolerance, and cooperation among Scouts from around the world.
- The 2019 Jamboree will be at the Summit Bechtel Reserve.

(5)
COMPARATIVE POLITICS

Note to Counselors: The boys were actually extremely into this section, most notably any time dictatorships came up. When North Korea, Communist countries, or historical examples from Nazi Germany, Stalinist Russia, etc. could be worked into the conversation, they became far more engaged.

In Appendix 2, there are lists of different countries, international agencies, and types of government. You can print these out and cut them into slips of paper to hand the boys, or create your own list. Ask them to answer questions based on the slips of paper they receive. For example, when discussing monarchies, ask who has a monarchy. This involves them more directly in the conversation and helps them really learn and retain at least one or two facts. In theory.

(A) DISCUSS THE DIFFERENCES BETWEEN CONSTITUTIONAL AND NON-CONSTITUTIONAL GOVERNMENTS.

In **constitutional governments**, power is usually limited by a written Constitution, but some nations have unwritten (or "uncodified") Constitutions.

- A **written Constitution** summarizes the basic law in one single written document, although amendments may be added later that change it. The United States has the oldest written national Constitution still in use.

- An **unwritten or uncodified Constitution** is when the law of a nation is based on a variety of written sources, laws, precedents, and customs instead of a single document. Great Britain is a modern example.

- Both the British and American systems include a Bill of Rights (1869 for Britain and 1789 for the USA, virtually simultaneous with the Constitution and a requirement for ratifying the Constitution in several states).

  Interestingly, British Common Law from before the American Revolution, when the states were British colonies, is still technically part of the American legal system.

- **Limited Power:** The **Rule of Law** says that the government and its officers may not exceed the limits of their power. They are subject to and not above the law.
  - The US Constitution specifies ways to remove offending officials from office (impeachment).
  - Removing them from office is different from criminal prosecution. It is similar to being fired from a job.
  - Impeached officials may face criminal charges, which is why President Ford officially pardoned President Nixon.

- **Higher Law:** The Constitution is the law of the land with no higher law above it.
  - **Individual rights** are protected from infringements by the government and other people. A "Bill of Rights" typically enumerates the most important protections, such as protections from illegal search and seizure.
  - **Limitations on power** are ensured by separating executive, legislative (writing laws), and judiciary (judging who has broken the law) powers using checks and balances.

- **Constitutional stability** means the Constitution cannot be changed without the consent of the citizens, often through their elected representatives, and requires the use of well-known, established amendment procedures to make changes.

  o Article V of the US Constitution includes two ways to amend it. The first is for the US Congress to pass an amendment and send it to the states for ratification, or approval. This method was used for all the amendments passed up through the 27th in 1992.

  o The second method is called an "Article V Convention." States may request Congress call a convention to amend the Constitution. Once two thirds of the states call for a Convention, Congress must call it and the state legislatures will select their delegates. Any amendments passed by the Convention will be sent to the states for ratification.

  Congress' only role is to actually call the Convention.

  o Three quarters of the US states must ratify any amendment for it to become part of the constitution no matter which method is used.

  o Technically, a Constitutional Convention is called to create, not modify, a Constitution. When people to call say there are calls for a Constitutional Convention to amend the US Constitution, they really mean an Article V Convention.

Many modern **non-Constitutional governments** are authoritarian. This means the authority to rule is concentrated in the hands of a single autocratic leader or a small group (oligarchy). Without checks and balances, a constitution to adhere to, or an electorate to please so they will vote for them, autocrats often act arbitrarily. The government rules without restraint or limitation. More variations are discussed below, in section 5b.

Constitutional

- A written Constitution provides stability.
- A constitution protects individual rights.
- Citizens are involved in lawmaking via elected representatives.
- Checks and balances encourage a more limited government.
- United States and Great Britain are examples.

Non-Constitutional

- These often lack stability and can change drastically with little warning.
- State's rights supersede individual rights.
- Only one or a few people are involved in law making.
- There are no restraints on government because there are no checks and balances.
- North Korea and Cuba are examples.

(B) NAME AT LEAST FIVE DIFFERENT TYPES OF GOVERNMENTS CURRENTLY IN POWER IN THE WORLD.

Some governments are one thing in theory and another in practice. Many autocracies are technically democracies, but in fact only the ruling party is on the voting ballots.

Autocracy: One ruler has unlimited power to govern. They could be a monarch, a dictator, or a military or religious leader.

Constitutional Monarchy: Constitutional governments with monarchs (King, Queen, Empress, Sultan, etc.) who may be either Ceremonial (United Kingdom, Canada) or active (Jordan, Qatar). Ceremonial monarchs do not have any power to make law. The British monarch can veto bills presented to her for signature, but it a major feature of British politics.

On the other hand, the Emir of Qatar has full executive powers and is extremely close to an absolute monarchy, but is still technically a constitutional monarch. In 2003, he granted families who were in the family prior to 1930 the right to vote and women can vote. Nonetheless, as of 2007, 75% of the population, including all foreign workers, was ineligible to vote.

Absolute Monarchy: The monarch has absolute power to govern. Modern examples include Saudi Arabia and, effectively, Kuwait. Kuwait is an example of a country that is one thing on paper but another in practice. In theory, it is a Constitutional Monarchy, but in practice it is an absolute monarchy because political organizations are illegal.

Oligarchy: Unlimited power to govern is in the hands of a few persons or a minority of the population, possibly a single political party. Russia is currently an oligarchy.

Junta: A military or political group that rules a country after taking power by force. Nigeria, Liberia, and Bolivia are just three examples.

Democracy: Unlimited power to govern is in the hands of the majority of the country's citizens. True democracies are rare, and small.

- **Direct Democracy:** The majority of citizens vote directly on all laws and other legislative issues. Ancient Rome was a direct democracy. The larger the population, the more unwieldy and difficult to maintain it is.

- **Representative Democracy:** For larger populations, particularly, electing representatives to vote for a certain block of citizens makes the process much smoother. The people's will is meant to be expressed indirectly through these elected representatives, as in the US House of Representatives. The US Senate is as well, as a result of the 1913 passage of the 17th Amendment.

Republic: Limited power to govern is in the hands of elected representatives. The United States was designed as a republic with Senators originally elected by state legislatures, not citizens.

Theocracy: A government ruled by the head of the ruling religion. Vatican City is a theocracy ruled by the Pope. It is nicknamed "the Papal City." Saudi Arabia, Qatar, and Iran are all effectively theocracies. (The head of the church and King/Queen can be the same person.)

(C) SHOW ON A WORLD MAP COUNTRIES THAT USE EACH OF THESE FIVE DIFFERENT FORMS OF GOVERNMENT.

(6)
FOREIGN AND INTERNATIONAL RELATIONS

(A) EXPLAIN HOW A GOVERNMENT IS REPRESENTED ABROAD AND HOW THE UNITED STATES GOVERNMENT IS ACCREDITED TO INTERNATIONAL ORGANIZATIONS.

The US Department of State works with foreign governments, international organizations, and people in other countries to bring them together into arrangements to promote peace, prosperity, and democratic governments.

> **Note:** The only time the noun "state" does not mean another nation is in reference to the 50 separate states of the USA. The Founders envisioned the states as having more power than the federal, or central government. In short, they expected them to virtually be their own nations (or "states") in many ways.
>
> This is why the Department of State deals with other nations, not the fifty states.

The **Department of State** has four main goals to make and carry out foreign policy:

- Protect the USA and her citizens.

- Advance economic prosperity, human rights, and other US interests in the world.
- Gain international understanding of American values and policies.
- Support US diplomats and government officials who work at home and abroad to make all this possible.

Full diplomatic relations include:

- Diplomatic recognition.
- Exchanging ambassadors.
- Establishing a full embassy with staff, normally in the capital city.
- Diplomatic immunity for foreign service/embassy staff.
    - Diplomatic immunity means foreign service officers (diplomats) are not subject to the laws of their host nation and cannot be arrested if they break the law.
    - This isn't meant to let people literally get away with murder, although that can happen. It exists to keep diplomats from being tossed in jail indefinitely for breaking minor, obscure or even contradictory laws, especially in countries run by dictators, juntas, etc.
    - It keeps diplomats out of jail when they are serving somewhere with a different political and judicial system than they have at home.

- Establishing consulates (see below, 6b) in larger nations.

Informal diplomacy is when a nation has an "Affairs Office" instead of an embassy.

- **Bhutan:** The US maintains relations through India, in New Delhi.
- **Iran:** Radical Islamic students stormed the US embassy in 1981 and took hostages because of US Support for the Shah of Iran. Since then, US and Iranian relations are conducted through the Swiss embassy.

- **N. Korea**
- **Taiwan:** Because China claims Taiwan as Chinese Taipei (their territory), most nations, including the US, have relations through the Taipei Economic and Cultural Republic Office rather than risking angering China.
- **Cuba:** The US had informal diplomacy with Cuba in opposition to their government, and as part of economic sanctions, for decades, but re-opened their embassy in Havana in 2015.

Virtual Presence Posts (VPPs) are the modern answer to nations where there is a barrier to keeping a traditional diplomatic presence. These barriers include small size (San Marino), danger (Somalia, Kenya), being part of a larger entity (Wales is part of Great Britain), and territorial disputes (Gaza).

- VPPs do not physically exist within the nation they represent and have no permanent officer.
- The first ones were established in 2006 and expanded in 2009 to a total of 50 worldwide in 2016.
- The Iranian VPP was established in 2011 in an attempt to provide information to Iranian citizens, but their government blocked their access.

(B) DESCRIBE THE ROLES OF THE FOLLOWING THE CONDUCT OF FOREIGN RELATIONS:

1. Ambassador:

- Top diplomat in country.
- Appointed by the President in the US.

2. Consul:

- Part of the Embassy Staff.
- Facilitates trade and friendship.
- Protects citizens while they are in foreign countries.

- Most (but not all) are in popular tourist cities so they can help tourists from their country who are in trouble.

3. Bureau of International Information Programs:

"The Bureau of International Information Programs (IIP) supports people-to-people conversations with foreign publics on U.S. policy priorities. To carry out this mission, IIP leverages digital communications technology to reach across platforms - from traditional forms of communications to new media channels. The bureau takes a strategic, data-driven approach to develop multimedia, digital communications products and to manage an overseas network of bricks-and-mortar American Spaces. Whether discussions take place in person or in virtual spaces, the bureau's top goal is to connect people with policy through dialogue that is relatable and understandable. In addition to IIP's ongoing programs, the bureau stands up timely special focus communications campaigns that respond to emerging issues."(from their website)

- This part of the US Department of State (IIP) connects people through policy.
- Their focus is on advancing US foreign policy goals directly with foreign audiences (the general public, media, government officials, and opinion leaders) in support of US embassies, consulates, and missions abroad.
- Their focus means they are involved with technology and social media.
- New Technology Camp provides help to entrepreneurs and women. It is also where the first Afghan Muppet received its voice.

4. US Agency for International Development (USAID):

- USAID is part of the US Department of State.

- USAID advances US foreign policy objectives by supporting economic growth, agriculture and trade (the three main pillars USAID is organized around), plus health, democracy, conflict prevention, and humanitarian aid.
- It provides assistance in Sub-Saharan Africa; Asia and the Near East; Latin America and the Caribbean; Europe; and Eurasia.
- It provides civilian foreign aid.
- USAID partners to end extreme poverty and promote resilient, democratic societies while advancing US security and prosperity.

5. United States and Foreign Commercial Service:

- The trade promotion arm of the International Trade Administration within the United States Department of Commerce.
- Mission:
  o To promote the export of goods and services from the United State, particularly by small and medium sized businesses;
  o To represent US business interests internationally; and
  o To help US businesses find qualified international partners.

(C) EXPLAIN THE PURPOSE OF A PASSPORT AND VISA FOR INTERNATIONAL TRAVEL.

Note to Counselors: If you are able to show the boys actual passports (redacted with personal information covered over in a photo copy works), this can really spark some interest. If you have more than one from different time periods, you can show the evolution of technology in passport production.

At one point, physical photos were attached. Later, they were laminated in. Later still, digital images replaced physical ones, security features were added, and now chips are embedded.

What is a Passport?

- A passport is a nationality and identity document usually granted only to a citizen or subject of the issuing country.
- A passport is used for identification and protection when traveling abroad.
- Passports include a photo, name, address, date of birth, and other personal information.
- A formal permit authorizing the holder to leave and return to the nation of which he or she is a citizen. In certain instances, the government takes their passport from a person accused of a crime to ensure they don't leave the country.
- Government officials often examine passports before allowing entry to their nation unless the nation has "open borders" and doesn't check passports.

What is a Visa?

- A formal endorsement government authorities place on a passport indicating that:
  - The passport has been examined and found valid by the nation to be visited, and
  - The bearer may legally go to his or her destination.

- In some cases, there are entry visas and exit visas and they must be obtained *before* travel starts.
- There are different kinds of visas, although immigrant and non-immigrant are the most basic kinds.
  - Some are temporary (tourism, education, business) and expire after a set period.

- o Work visas may be indefinite, lasting as long as the bearer remains employed by the same company, or term-limited, based on a specific task or contract.
- o Educational visas are a separate class from the visitor visas used for short visits. Students must be accepted by a school or exchange program before applying for a Visa.

- Visas are for a set period and they expire.
  - o Anyone wishing to remain in a country must renew their visa, which the host nation is not required to do.
  - o Governments may check on visa holders to ensure they are following the rules established for their stay.

(7)
LEARN ABOUT OTHER CULTURES

Note to Counselors: This particular requirement is often done outside of class because three of the five options involve physically visiting somewhere. Because the remaining two involve going online, they may require parental permission or supervision.

Do TWO of the following and share with your counselor what you have learned:

a. Visit the Web site (With your parent/guardian's permission) of the U.S. State Department (https://www.state.gov). Learn more about an issue you find interesting that is discussed on this Web site.

(The front page has recent news stories. There is also an entire section on "Policy Issues" for you to explore.)

b. Visit the Web site (With your parent/guardian's permission) of an international news organization or foreign government, OR examine a foreign newspaper available at your local library, bookstore, or newsstand. Find a news story about a human right realized in the United States that is not recognized in another country.

c. Visit with a student or Scout from another country and discuss the typical values, holidays, ethnic foods, and traditions practiced or enjoyed there.

d. Attend a world Scout jamboree.

e. Participate in or attend an international event in your area, such as an ethnic festival, concert, or play.

Appendix 1: Resources on Comparing North and South Korea

1. South v North Korea: how do the two countries compare? Visualized
   https://www.theguardian.com/world/datablog/2013/apr/08/south-korea-v-north-korea-compared

2. South Korea vs North Korea
   http://www.indexmundi.com/factbook/compare/south-korea.north-korea

3. A Crazy Comparison Of Life In North Korea And South Korea
   http://www.businessinsider.com/life-in-north-korea-vs-south-korea-2013-4

4. The differences between South and North Korea explained
   https://www.scenesofreason.com/north-korea-explained/

5. The Stark Difference Between North And South Korea In 10 Stunning Photos
   http://www.huffingtonpost.com/2014/05/29/dieter-leistner-korea-photos_n_5405585.html

6. Some North Korean Refugees Are So Depressed By Their Life In The South That They Go Back North
   http://www.businessinsider.com/some-north-korean-refugees-are-so-depressed-by-their-life-in-the-south-that-they-go-back-north-2012-8

7. Juche
   https://en.wikipedia.org/wiki/Juche

8. North and South Korea: how different are they?
   http://www.dw.com/en/north-and-south-korea-how-different-are-they/a-17996315

9. The Striking Differences Between North and South Korea Summed Up in 22 Eye-Opening Photos

http://www.distractify.com/old-school/2014/12/29/difference-between-north-and-south-korea-1197802378

10. North Korean vs South Korean Economies
    http://www.investopedia.com/articles/forex/040515/north-korean-vs-south-korean-economies.asp

APPENDIX 2: NATIONS AND AGENCIES

Saudi Arabia

Great Britain

Somalia

France

Australia

Canada

Germany

Russia

The Soviet Union

Taiwan

China

Monaco

Vatican City

The United Kingdom

Qatar

Iran

Iraq

Cuba

Afghanistan

Pakistan

India

Guam

Mexico

European Union

The World Court

UNICEF

USAid

The World Bank

The UN

The World Bank

INTER-POL

NATO

ABOUT THE AUTHOR

Bethanne Kim is a life-long Scout. She joined Girl Scouts in 1st grade and became a lifetime member at 21. Naturally, she only had boys, leading to her not-inconsiderable involvement in Boy Scouts.

Kim cares enough about Scouting that she not only agreed to be a Girl Scout troop Leader for girls in a county run half-way house, but to be an Assistant Leader for a troop locked up in juvi. They counted the pencils when the leaders entered and left, no pens allowed in jail, and the meeting area was surrounded by the girls' cells.

Her long list of Girl Scout accomplishments in, including earning the Gold Award, are one reason she was called on to become involved in Boy Scouts. She was a Cubmaster for four years, Assistant Cubmaster for two, and is currently an Assistant Scoutmaster and active member of the District leadership. Kim now has her PhD in Cub Scouting from Scout University and has taken enough classes in Boy Scouting to be a PhD Candidate in that, and it taking Wood Badge. She has been the ASM for New Scouts in a boy-led troop of over 80 boys, including over twenty new Scout, and is now the ASM for a brand new unit of nine that had two boys when she signed on.

Outside of Scouts, Kim earned her Bachelor's degree in International Studies from Johns Hopkins University, and is the happily married mom of two. She keeps busy building a website for dads (WiseFathers.com), blogging at TheModerateMom.com, and writing and promoting books.

Please take a minute to look at all her other books and to review this one on Amazon.

Other Books

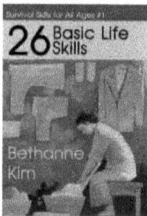

Survival Skills for All Ages Book 1: Basic Life Skills covers skills so simple most emergency preparedness books skip right over them. In true emergencies, knowing how to sharpen kitchen knives and basic sanitation can be literal life savers. Skills were chosen for their value in everyday life as well as emergencies.

Survival Skills for All Ages Book 2: 52+ Everyday Recipes for Emergencies is chock full of recipes that can be cooked either on or off-grid. That means that during a power outage, on a camping trip, or any other time you want or need to cook without power, you can continue to enjoy the same meals you normally have.

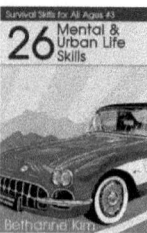

Survival Skills for All Ages Book 3: 26 Mental & Urban Life Skills covers financial skills, staying safe while traveling, self-defense, cyber security, hiding from danger, handling your emotions (including stress and anger), and more. These skills can help kids and adults throughout life, not just in school.

Cubmastering: Getting Started as Cubmaster is an introduction for new Cubmasters. Topics covered include organizational structure, training, recruiting, and recharter. This is about more than just the nuts and bolts of Scouting, though. It also covers dealing with difficult parents and planning special pack events.

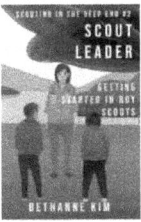

Scout Leader: An Introduction to Boy Scouts focuses on the nuts and bolts of Cub Scouts. Unit organization and BSA organization are both explained, as is recharter and the common BSA meetings (such as Roundtable) and trainings. Each chapter starts with a quote from Lord Baden Powell.

OMG! Not the Zombies! Book 1 A group of teens goes for a hike and accidentally starts the zombie apocalypse. Being good at being prepared, they start setting up a safe community in the old Indian cliff houses and stocking it with supplies to save themselves and their families while the adults are still pretending life is normal.

BRB! Not the Zombies! Book 2 As their group grows, they discover a new mission: Get crucial information and items to the CDC to help with efforts to create a cure for the Infection. They fight their way through zombie-infested towns and to find the "impregnable" CDC research station their hopes are pinned on.

Swept Away: Mother Nature vs. the Zombies Not the Zombies! Book 3 Have you ever wondered how a hurricane might affect the zombie apocalypse? Or how the undead would fare in a sandstorm? (Hint: Hope they aren't wearing a helmet.) These and other natural disasters are explored in this series of short stories set in the same zombie apocalypse as *OMG! Not the Zombies!*

The Organized Wedding: Planning Everything from Your Engagement to Your Marriage is chock full of checklists. No detail is too small! What truly sets it apart is including the actual wedding ceremony and a chapter on your marriage with questions on financial priorities, family health history, and all your doctors.

FORTHCOMING:

Survival Skills for All Ages: 26 Outdoor Life Skills covers all kinds of camping skills such as knot tying, fire building, outdoor cooking, and choosing a tent. It also covers hunting, fishing, and foraging for food; finding your way using maps, compasses, and GPSs; and truly basic skills such as managing time and water safety (tides, currents, etc.).

Survival Skills for All Ages: Special Needs Prepping may sound like something only "other people" need but the truth is that most families have special needs. Babies, elderly parents, diabetes, asthma, allergies – most of us have at least one of these and even if we don't, a simple sprained ankle or back injury can make us (temporarily) special needs.

Emergency preparedness can be tough, but it's even harder when someone in your family has special needs. A lot of these are surprisingly common, such as being dependent on medication ranging from an asthma inhaler or epi-pen to tightly controlled narcotics. Others, such as mobility impairment, can be long-term or short-term like a sprained ankle. Mental challenges, food allergies, diabetes, elder care, small children…. There is a lot to cover in one book

YOLO! Not the Zombies! Book 3 Follow them into the Great Plains and Texas as they continue searching not just for other survivors and their own friends and family, but for any CDC facilities that can still help fight the virus.

CONTACT THE AUTHOR

Bethanne would love to hear from you! You can connect with her through:

Blogs–TheModerateMom.com; WiseFathers.com

Email–theWiseMom@WiseFathers.com

Facebook–The Moderate Mom

Pinterest–TheModerateMom

Twitter–@TheModerateMom

Because Amazon reviews really do matter, especially for indie authors, please take a few minutes and post a review of this book on Amazon.com.

www.ingramcontent.com/pod-product-compliance
Lightning Source LLC
Chambersburg PA
CBHW071343290326
41933CB00040B/2167